Copyright © 2022

Wildflower
By
Ibura Ayele

Notice of Copyright

All rights reserved. No part of this publication may be reproduced, distributed, or transmitted in any form or by any means, including photocopying, recording, or other electronic or mechanical methods, without the prior written permission of the publisher, except in the case of brief quotations embodied in critical reviews and certain other non-commercial uses permitted by copyright law. For permission requests, write to the publisher, addressed "Attention: Permissions Coordinator," at the address below.

Printed By:
Fifth Ribb Publishing Company
6951 Olive Blvd.
University City, MO 63130

Printed in the United States of America

First Printing Edition, 2022
ISBN 9-781736-789827

Wildflower

by Ibura Ayele

Illustrated by Sarah Blair

*For my fearless mother/best friend/superhero,
I love you deeper than the ocean and higher than the sky.*

Contents

Preface	8
Mental Health Resources	11

THE WOMAN

Wildflower	14
freedom as work in progress	15
Love Language	16
Baptism	17
Tongues	18
4216 Clarence Ave.	19
Spiders	20

THE GRIEF

new	22
7 things my therapist didn't tell me	23
Music Therapy in 4 Noname Lyrics	24
Visions of a Bereaved Daughter	26
miracle	27
Psalm 30:5	28
Okay	29
Ubuntu	30
5.26.20 – journal entry	31
Weathering (you will not kill me, too)	32
Nostalgia	34
Solitude	35
Trudge On	36

THE LEGACY AND HOW WE GO ON

Strength	38
Love	39
Return to Self	40
My Prayer	41
Stay	42
Growing Pains	43
When it Manifests	44
dream girl part I	45
dream girl part II	46
Postcard to Heaven	47
black girl, fly on	48
REFERENCES	50
ACKNOWLEDGEMENTS	51
ABOUT THE AUTHOR	52

"I write because I am a rebel and I want others like me to know they are not alone."
– Sherri Rich[1]

---

[1] Sherri Rich was my mother's stage name for part of her career as a singer/songwriter. This quote comes from a version of her "About" page on her former website.

Preface

I lost my mom to breast cancer in September 2017. The summer of 2018 was my first summer without her, and I was turning 20. It was the summer after my freshman year of college and my first taste of adulting. Throughout the summer, I worked three jobs, volunteered weekly, shadowed in the ER, was involved in a "situationship," drank— and did just about anything I could to distract myself and avoid my grief. But somehow, through it all, my mother still reached out to comfort me.

One early morning on my way to work, I was exiting the highway and in the grass along the median little flashes of purple caught my eye. I would later learn that these were chicory flowers, which are technically blue, but in the sun they have a purple tint. Purple was my mom's favorite color, and in 2016 I began writing about my mother using wildflower imagery because of the grit and determination she showed during her battle with cancer. From the instant I saw these flowers bathed in the gentle morning sunlight, I knew it was my mom letting me know that she was alright and that she loved me.

At one of my jobs, I spent a lot of time outside canvassing neighborhoods in St. Louis City. While walking up and down different blocks passing out flyers, and during my commutes between jobs, I saw these wildflowers constantly. They mostly grew in the vacant lots around the neighborhoods we canvassed and along the side of the highway. The sight of those flowers comforted me that summer and has every summer since by reminding me that my mom is always with me.

I started writing about my grief later that summer, and throughout the following months I fell into depression and social anxiety. Once I was finally able to talk about my grief and the tailspin that my summer-of-avoidance threw me into, I got into therapy and I began to face it all. I continue to work through the depression every day. Although I never stop missing my mom, each day gets easier as I continue to grow into the woman I am meant to be.

In therapy, I learned about the five stages of grief: denial, anger, bargaining, depression, and acceptance. The stages are not necessarily meant to be a linear progression, but rather, a way of describing the range of emotions one experiences while grieving. I experience grief as a tangled web of these stages, though these emotions are less intense now as time has helped to dull the pain. At the time, learning about the stages of grief helped me make sense of a lot of the anguish I was feeling. For example, at some points I felt like if I had been a better caregiver maybe I could have made my mom more comfortable in her final days. Other times, I fumed about the people and situations in her life that caused her immense stress and blamed them for her diagnosis and ultimately her death. I also found myself angry with God and struggled with my faith.

Being able to understand and categorize some of the thoughts I was having was helpful. But I found that writing about my mom's life made me feel as if she hadn't died for nothing. I wanted her to live on through my words, so I journaled and wrote poetry to process my grief and to try to capture my mom's essence. Over the years, there have been times where writing poems for her was all I could do, where it was what I had to do to rise from grief.

David Kessler, an expert on death and dying, describes this as the sixth stage: finding meaning. Kessler was a student and friend of Elisabeth Kübler-Ross, the psychiatrist who originally identified the five stages of grief. In his book, Finding Meaning: The Sixth Stage of Grief, he writes, "in this sixth stage we acknowledge that although for most of us grief will lessen in intensity over time, it will never end. But if we allow ourselves to move fully into this crucial and profound sixth stage—meaning—it will allow us to transform grief into something else, something rich and fulfilling," (17).

There's no due date for finding meaning, and it will look different for everyone. For me, finding meaning doesn't mean I'm done hurting, but it is a beautiful way for me to love my mom and remember her life. It feels a lot better than drowning in depression. Though its waters still lap at my ankles, it is finally bearable. Kessler writes, "[l]oss can wound and paralyze. It can hang over us for years. But finding meaning in loss empowers us to find a path forward," (17). Loss is something that everyone will experience during their time here on Earth and I think finding meaning for ourselves makes us stronger, more compassionate individuals.

Wildflower is a part of my journey in finding meaning. It is a love letter to my mother and our family. It is my heart on a page. This book is my pain, my poetry, and the power I've found in the healing process. Healing can be messy and uncomfortable. I pray that readers find comfort in my words as they embark on their healing journeys. Know that in your pain, there is softness and love still, because souls never die.

Love and light,

Ibura Ayele

Mental Health Resources

- Call the Suicide & Crisis Lifeline (988) to be connected with a trained counselor anytime.

- Crisis Text Line: Text HOME to 741-741 to connect with a counselor 24/7

- Grief and Loss Resources via the American Counseling Association:
  https://www.counseling.org/knowledge-center/mental-health-resources/grief-and-loss-resources

Resources for Finding a Therapist:
- Therapy for Black Girls Directory:
  https://providers.therapyforblackgirls.com
- Psychology Today Directory:
  https://www.psychologytoday.com/us
- Therapy for Black Men Directory:
  https://therapyforblackmen.org/therapists/
- National Queer & Trans Therapists of Color Network:
  https://nqttcn.com/en/mental-health-directory/
- Online Therapy
  https://openpathcollective.org

Financial Support for Therapy Sessions:
- The Loveland Foundation Therapy Fund:
  https://thelovelandfoundation.org

Resources for depression:
- Anxiety & Depression Association of America:
  https://adaa.org

THE WOMAN

"Cowards have no idea what it's like to be free,
So, you can't imagine what it's like being me."
- Sherri Rich

Wildflower

During summertime, in our hood, purple wildflowers grow by sidewalks, in the untamed yards of abandoned buildings and vacant plots.
Their beauty is unapologetic. No matter how the ugly history of racism and disenfranchisement looms over in the form of dilapidated buildings and stares up through the cracked pavement. There is beauty still. Don't mistake them for weeds just because they grow fiercely. We call anything we can't control a weed. They are flowers. They bloom and prosper for their own glory.
Mama was a wildflower.
Unapologetic in beauty and stance.
Free.

freedom as work in progress

Everyone admired my mother for her free spirit.
I studied bravery by watching her navigate a world that undervalues the artists
that keep our hearts afloat through the worst of times.
She taught me that misery was too high a price to pay for security.
That passion projects are vital, and dreams are a worthy investment.

Even when finances were fickle, every moment with her felt like an adventure.
She strutted through life in fabulous high-heels sharing her talents freely and
followed her interests down whatever winding road they took her.
I am still learning how to show up in spaces as my full self,
inviting others to like it— or not,
and how to pivot when I reach a dead-end.

Together, we dreamt wildly of inventions, projects, and businesses to come.
Most never came to be. Many lived and died in a season.
The most beautiful part of it all being, how much we believed in each other.

That's what set us free.

Love Language

Mommy's love language was balloons from the dollar store.
Color-coordinated, of course, tied-up outside the party
to let everyone passing by know that she's happy you're alive.
Her joy for giving was palpable and overflowing
like the gift bags she stuffed with pink tissue paper.

For her, love was not only grand displays of affection
but also, a practice of daily affirmation.
I love you's, bedtime check-ins, and pep talks were routine.
Encouraging notes would find themselves tucked in my lunch box
—always with silly sketches, mostly stick figures.

She spoke in care packages, cakes, handmade gifts, and surprises.
She wrote in poems, song lyrics, and sappy letters.
She loved out loud.
She spelled it in plastic paints, icing, or marker,
so you could see plainly in color,
hear, feel, and know
that you were loved.

Baptism

"I sing because it feels good, natural and necessary for me to fill my body with the sound of my voice until it overflows, making my every cell dance and vibrate."
– Sherri Rich

All my life I was bathed in music.
The sound of my mother's voice painted the walls of each new home.
As she practiced for gigs, belted out a love song, grieved the loss of her father,
or lulled me to sleep—waves of song flowed from one room to the next,
cleansing the space like sage, assuring me that I was safe.

Like a baby bird learning to sing,
I filled my tiny body with notes and released them to the best of my ability.
Often pausing to laugh and clear my throat,
I learned to harmonize just enough to join the songbird
in her ritual of taking up space with sound.
That freeing act of baptizing a space with the power of your voice.

Tongues
after Frank X Walker

I used to tease mommy for what we called her "Buffy voice"
Her conducting business, reporting, parent-teacher conferencing,
sounds kinda like an email looks—voice.

D as in door,
E as in elephant,
H as in house,
A,
A,
N as in Nancy,
is how I learned to spell my last name, overhearing her phone calls.

Around me her voice was warm,
but careful
not to slip too far into the northside accent she was raised with,
careful,
to pronounce my name in all its glory, so I'd know to correct people
when I heard it butchered by the knives we Americans carry in our mouths.

I loved the rare times I heard her R's relax to melt words like
her, hair, & here
into an indistinguishable one, the way only Saint Louisans can.

Around her sisters she was class clown,
twisting and bending language like
balloon animals,
making everyone burst with laughter.

Around our family her tongue was colorful,
bright as her smile,
and loud as she wanted to be.

4216 Clarence Ave.

At home there was always nachos—made our way.
There was sure to be a TV on in the evenings and a warm place to binge-watch.
At home Sunday mornings were for pancakes and turkey sausage and eggs.
At home there was art on the walls and music mingled with incense in the air.
There, random bursts into song were not only welcome, but encouraged
and our kitchen tile was good as any ballroom floor.
At home the dining table was decoration,
for the finest meals were to be served on our laps.
At home we found quiet when we needed it.
On our couch, we took refuge from the world
by escaping into well-needed nap.

At home life felt simple, even when it wasn't.
Even when the world shook our foundation,
we stood together, sheltered and safe.

Spiders

I knew something was different about me when my cousin woke me up at 2am to kill a spider and I did it with no hesitation.

Mommy taught me how to kill spiders through a sort of exposure therapy. At first she'd kill them for me. Then, she'd stand in the room until I stopped screaming long enough to kill one myself. Later, she wouldn't even come to look at the thing terrorizing me. I had to get over the squeamishness and paralyzing fear, then handle it. I killed spiders, crickets, centipedes, and all kinds of unwanted guests living in our old-ass city apartments.

I think she anticipated the day that she wouldn't be around to squash my fears for me. So, she taught me to look fear in the face and see how small it is

to recognize how powerful I am.

THE GRIEF

"If there ever comes a day when we can't be together,
keep me in your heart, I'll stay there forever."
—Winnie the Pooh

n e w

Death is hard.
Hard to talk about, hard to comfort.
Hard for us to comprehend
 the absence. The empty room,
leftover clothes and shoes.
All the belongings too sacred to touch.
Every time I go somewhere without you for the first time
I make a mental note.
For fear that if I don't,
I'll start to forget that this is all strange to me,
being here, without you.
Like if this becomes normal, somehow, I lose a piece of you.

7 things my therapist didn't tell me

1. Language gets harder. Oscillating between denial and acceptance and just plain habit. You'll wish there was some imperfect in-between because the past burns the back of your throat—was.
It's too final. It falls on the air like concrete and you'll wish you could pick it back up and stuff it down deep. But the present feels like a lie—she is, no, she was.

2. You'll never be able to tell her stories just right. The punch lines won't land the same way.

3. You'll burst out laughing in public at inside jokes that are now one-sided.

4. Her opinions will leap out of your mouth masked as your own.

5. You'll start keeping a mental note when you go someplace without her for the first time, and you might cry in Whole Foods.

6. Eventually you'll lose track.

7. No one's caramel cake will ever taste just like hers.

Music Therapy in 4 Noname Lyrics

"The secret is, I'm actually broken" [1]

heart is jagged and stained
my smile is plastered and frozen
body a mosaic of pain.

hold it, hold it together.

they called me pretty the day we said goodbye to her.
eyes skimmed over a spirit drained
really felt like a double-sided mirror,
inside only half a heart remained.

hold it, hold it together.

*"When the sun is going down and the dark is out to stay,
I picture your smile, like it was yesterday"* [2]

The funny thing about yesterday
is it keeps changing,
its never here to stay,
pictures fading, memories rearranging.

Yesterday, we were walking down the street,
Ted Drew's in one hand, your arm in the other,
Autumn leaves crunching under our feet.
I could've never dreamt of a world without my mother.

Sometimes yesterday is a car ride,
blasting Coldplay, flying down the highway,
me at your side,
in a timeless moment, a world of our own.

---

[1] Fatimah Warner, Jon Pierre-Louis, Michael Anthony Neil. "Don't Forget About Me." *Room 25*. Noname, 2018.
[2] Fatimah Warner. "Yesterday." *Telefone*. Noname, 2016.

*"Everybody think they know me,
Don't nobody really know me"* ³

Mommy used to tell stories of life before me
like, *don't you remember when…?*
only to recall I wasn't born.
Said, she felt like I was always with her back then,
as if we'd been here as friends before.

I used to feel like couldn't nobody really know me
unless they knew us, together.
But as each year blurs into the next,
I wonder if she'd recognize me still.

I lost myself clinging to a lover
that would only embrace me in the dark.
Now, I'm trying to get to know me.

*"They ain't tryna see us shine, shine
Bullet on our time, time
But, fuck it, we'll live forever"* ⁴

My mama said she could talk to the weather.
She'd make the rain slow to a drizzle
long enough to take the groceries inside.

Mama talked to God on the regular,
said she sent up prayers for me.
Even bargained with God for me
said, *God please let this child be healthy,
I don't even care if she can't sing like me.*

She must've had a direct line cause I was her miracle baby
and I sholl can't sing like her.
I know she's somewhere laughing, kickin' it with the angels.

---

3 Brian Sanborn, Fatimah Warner, Jon Pierre-Louis, Luke Sangerman, Michael Anthony Neil. "Window (ft. Phoenix)." *Room 25*. Noname, 2018.
4 Fatimah Warner, Joseph Chilliams, Michael Neil, Ravyn Lenae, Tahj Chandler. "Forever (ft. Ravyn Lenae & Joseph Chilliams)." *Telefone*. Noname, 2016.

Visions of a Bereaved Daughter

My mama lives in the sun.
She moved away and left me on an alien planet, that looks so familiar.
Here, cloudy days are the hardest.
Sometimes it's so cold, I just can't get out of bed.

Ever since, I've been sending her up messages in spaceships.
She gave life to me and now she gives life to everything,
and she must be the reason my heart hasn't frozen over yet.
My dreams make her feel like she never left.

Her rays warm my skin and make the flowers bloom.
Though she is 93 million miles away,
I can see her face so clearly in my dreams.
Sometimes I storm, I tornado, I hurricane

because these 93 million miles are agonizing.
But I know the sun shines with the same radiance behind the clouds.
I'm learning to keep my storms inside while I look for silver linings.
My mama lives in the sun and she rises anew each morning.

m i r a c l e

They say electrons are just waves of probability
that collapse into one possibility as soon as an observer looks.
I wonder, did the wine turn back to water when the drinks stopped pouring?

They named me "Miracle of God."
What do you call a miracle that's lost its faith?
A disappointment?
What am I when no one's looking?

Psalm 30:5

Joy is supposed to come in the morning,
but the bitch is always late.
I don't know how to tell my professor the reason I wasn't in class was because I was waiting—
that I laid in bed all day waiting for her.

Okay

I awake. I speak softly, so as not to scare away the happy thoughts, I hope they'll stay a while. It's been storming so long, but I found the calm. There is softness, there is love here. I should have been shipwrecked, but the waters are still, and I'm still afloat. I look up to soft pink skies. I can see joy on the horizon. I've got some hope in my back pocket for later. Today will be okay.

Ubuntu

You are stronger than you feel in this moment.
Your mother powers every cell in your body, as do all the women before her.
There is a tribe, a village, a home,
purpose, power, strength, and love—all pumping through your veins.
You were made for this.
Ancestors strengthen your body and spirit.
I am because we are.

5.26.20 – journal entry

I feel like I don't have room to grieve in this world environment right now. I also don't have it in me to hold any more anger or anguish for those lost. It feels hard to be in this skin right now. To hurt for all the violence against black bodies as it manifests medically, systemically, physically. It's a lot to hold and my arms feel full. To scroll past memes and then see a black man's face on pavement, a white man kneeling on his neck. Nobody's family should have to see that. It just brings me to tears. Hot, angry, tired, and horrified tears. I'm glad I'm not desensitized too much yet.

Weathering (you will not kill me, too)

"My sister died fighting for justice…You won't kill me"
- Emerald Snipes, Daughter of Eric Garner

Stress is killing our mamas.
To be Black and woman
and strong and struggling
in a society that will never
see us as worthy
                of protection
or compassion
                or justice,
it wears away at you,
                pulls piece by piece,
block by block until
Jenga. You fall
ill
under pressure that
has built over the years.

                you will not kill me, too

                I will return to myself each day to
                       rest   restore   recover
                         from the storm outside,
                            the weathering.

I will

    love who I want   laugh till I cry & heave for air   *(then laugh some more)*

   smile with my mama's smile   dance with limbs long like my daddy's

     heal   resist   dream   learn   & unlearn

    build new futures   pray over my village

I rest to honor ancestors (known and unknown)

    Sherry Haynes-DeHaan   Erica Garner
                  Audre Lorde

Fannie Lou Hamer   Octavia Butler
         Nina Simone

and all those who lived in pursuit of the freedom to be Black and woman and *radically* free

Nostalgia

Won't you tell me how to get
back to the pitter patter of baby feet,
bananas and baby meat.
Back when we all had Teletubby tummies.
Back to playground mulch
making way for light-up shoes coming through.
Back to chalk on sidewalk– and chalk all over our clothes.
Back to blowing bubbles big as our heads,
and running through grass with bare feet.
Back to playdates with imaginary friends and
checking under the bed for imaginary monsters,
cause these days
the monsters be too real.

> "In a world that entices us to browse through the lives of others to help us better determine how we feel about ourselves, and to in turn feel the need to be constantly visible, for visibility these days seems to somehow equate to success—do not be afraid to disappear from it, from us for a while, and see what comes to you in the silence."
> —Michaela Coel, Emmy Awards 2021

Solitude

when I'm feeling brave,
I sit in silence to hear the poetry.
I let the feelings overtake me
until they writhe into words.

most times, I scroll through the static,
placing distance between me
and the pain. more noise.
all day. running. scrolling.
then sleep. shut out thoughts,
holding eyelids closed tight.
wake up to scroll through what I've missed.

solitude is heavy.
I sink down down down till my pen
brings my head above water once again.
I float alone in the silence,
and I begin to hear the poetry.

Trudge On

My feet move through the slush on my way to the bus.
Not quite snow, not quite water, an annoying in-between
it makes room for my boots, as snowflakes form blurs of water on my
glasses. There's something reassuring about seeing breath mingle with
winter air.
I rest in my seat knocking water from my feet,
knowing I've done
a good thing.
And I think,
Maybe I can do this.
Maybe it won't
always be so hard.
Maybe this life
will make room
for a me without you.
For you, I'll trudge on
      through the slush
           vision blurred
                blindly trusting
                    that one day,
                          I'll see you on the other side.

THE LEGACY AND HOW WE GO ON

"Souls don't die"
-The Iron Giant

Strength

I've seen Strength in the flesh.
She's a Black woman,
with ten times as many problems
as kinks & curls in her afro
But you'd never know.
Her backbone is made of platinum,
and her heart is encased in gold.
And man— she looked just like my mama.

I sat down with Strength the other day
for what I thought was the first time.
But she told me I'd known her my whole life.

She'd lived in my mama's smile.
The one that shone down on you
the way the sun peeks through the clouds after a hurricane.
Peace in the midst of chaos.
An infectious smile,
That grabbed onto your leg like a child might,
and only held on tighter when you tried to shake it off.

I've seen glimpses of her in my mama's eyes,
Those eyes that still twinkled with joy
after years of adversity,
because diamonds had formed beneath their surface.

I've heard Strength in her voice.
That voice that proved my mama was an angel,
And that God had simply lent her to us
to love on this plane for a time.

Now our angel has returned to the Father,
But she has left her legacy and her strength with me.
I can tell, because now everyone says
we look just alike.

Yes, I've seen Strength in the flesh,
 and she looks just like my mama.

Love

I come from Great Migration descendants and Caribbean immigrants,
from buffalo soldiers and dreadlock rastas,
from sweet potato pie and fried plantain.
Jill Scott and Bob Marley co-wrote the soundtrack to my childhood
singing of love and pride.

I was taught love by warrior women.
By women who the world ain't give no choice but to be strong,
but they did so with grace and a touch of magic.
They mixed love into my oatmeal until it grew me up like a bean stalk.

I come from women of faith.
Granny said Jesus loved me and armed me with rosaries,
while mama whispered her prayers for me into God's ear.
I went to Catholic school during the week and to Baptist church on Sundays,
Black *and* white Jesus love me.

I was taught love through joanin' sessions.
I was taught love is a verb, love is unashamed.
Love always texts to see if you got home safe.

It looks like dancing in the kitchen,
it feels like climbing into my mama's bed at the end of a hard day,
because love takes you as you are
(but you better change outta yo street-clothes first).

Love knows what you need before you do.
It fusses at you when your elbows are on the table
or when your glasses are dirty.

Don't tell me what love looks like, I've met her.
You don't know her like I do.
Your love is bittersweet,
and I won't settle for anything less than sweet potato pie.

Return to Self

my family calls me "tree" cause I sprouted up fast. limbs branching out long.
I soak up sun. I make my own food.
I consume poems to survive, and I've been starving.
the name of this poem is no, thank you
is more me please
is no more
is chapter closed
is book thrown out the window
is fuck closure.
I will name this poem fresh start.
a return to forever finding myself, who was here all along.
I will dance it and sing it and scream it to the sky.
I will name this poem redemption song.
I will name this poem after myself. I will name it enough.
the name of this poem is free at last.
I will whisper it into my palms and wield it as a sword against my darkness.
it will dry my tears. it will weep with me.
the name of this poem is no, thank you, I am enough and will always be more than enough.
the name of this poem is full.
this poem is love.

My Prayer

I've surrendered to the fact that we all become our mothers in the end.
To this day, I'll never sit my purse on the floor.
Won't take my heels off at a party.
She invades my thoughts when I see a smoker
Fire on one end, fool on the other.

We can't help but be conscious of the things they fussed about,
get your shoes out the middle of the floor.
Can't help but recant their jokes as our own
Better practice walking in heels, these girls out here walking like tarantulas.
You wanna study abroad? What broad??

Not quite sure where my mama ends and I begin.

I pray we inherit their wisdom, strength, light, and learn from their pain.
I pray that their sorrow does not reside in our hearts.
Heartbreak has helped me to empathize with my mama in a new way.
I understand how love can make you crazy.
Especially when you settle for less than you deserve.

I pray that we hold ourselves accountable to only accept the best love,
while showing ourselves extraordinary love, care, and forgiveness.
I pray we heal our trauma, and that our mothers might heal through us too.
I pray we love our communities fiercely, love our sisters dearly, and build new worlds together.

Stay

I'm learning how to stay.
Stay for the night, stay to talk it out, stay calm,
be still.

How do I still my spirit without becoming stagnant?
Or paralyzed by fear?

I'm learning how to ride the wave and trust these waters.
I know the sharks circling beneath are only in my memory.

I'm learning how to stay in it and feel the love that's growing day by day.
This love needs me to stay a while and water it.

I'm in love and I'm learning how to stay here.
How to bask in the warmth of a good thing
and thank God for these clear skies.

Growing Pains

Today I want to be green instead of gray.
I'll adorn myself in emeralds and feel the grass between my toes.
If I am green today,
I can play leapfrog with my worries and dance under the evergreens.
Let me be green today,
find solace in Gethsemane under the olive trees,
so I can be Earth and garden and new.
So I can be rooted.

May I grow.
Though I feel like falling apart,
Grace sustains me.
I know, this too, shall pass.
And soon, I will be green.

When it Manifests

and when they ask you how you did it,
I hope you'll smile
with sunshine in your cheeks
and tell them
that you weathered storms and
climbed through jungles to arrive here.

remember to tell them how dark it was.
how you couldn't see past your next footstep,
but you kept going.

and how your vision
was the only thing lighting your path.

dream girl part I

I am not your dream girl,
But I am a dream.
Mama always said I was the girl of her dreams.
She said she saw my face and wild hair
while I was still dreaming in her womb.

Wake up
I am not your dream girl,
your snow globe,
your trophy,
your model,
your conquest.
This magic can be neither captured nor shelved.

Hello, nice to meet you.
I'm not what you're looking for,
but I sure am a treasure.
And I can't be nobody but me, for me.
Ever-changing.

dream girl part II

I don't daydream often, but when I do, I can see her.
I see my unborn daughter's round face and brown skin shining with Vaseline.
Shiny cracker-crumb teeth, a little purple sundress, black curls defying gravity.
She has my apple cheeks, his smile, and bright, loving eyes.

I bet she'll laugh loud and freely like my daddy
throwing her head back, consumed with joy.
I bet she'll be able to work a room full of people like my mama
generously sharing her talents.
Maybe she'll have my goofy sense of humor.
Maybe one day she'll reintroduce herself to us and choose her own name.
I know she'll have an intellect and style that's all her own.

I've not met her, but when I do, I know she'll dance into my arms, her soul
gleaming with a familiar light. Awe-struck, I'll smile and think,
I've known you forever.

Postcard to Heaven

black girl, fly on

a queen, always been too big for her body. too big for this world.
black girl, fly on.
i was always under your wing,
dancing in your shadow,
now I gotta learn to fly on my own.
black girl, fly on
past the horizon, painted purple just for you.
may the wind be at your back, as you soar into the heavens,
and we wonder if it was all just a magnificent dream.
black girl, fly on
leaving a whirlwind of music and glitter in your wake.
fly on to greet all those we've loved and those we've yet to meet.
make a place for us,
up there beyond the clouds
black girl, fly on

REFERENCES

Preface

    Kessler, David. *Finding Meaning: The Sixth Stage of Grief*. E-book, Simon & Schuster, Inc. 2019.

"Tongues"

    Walker, Frank X. "Talking in Tongues." *Ink Stains & Watermarks: New and Uncollected Poems*. Print. Duncan Hills Press, 2017.

"Weathering (you will not kill me, too)"

    Demby, Gene. "Making The Case That Discrimination Is Bad For Your Health." *The Code Switch Podcast*, NPR, 14 Jan. 2018. https://www.npr.org/sections/codeswitch/2018/01/14/577664626/making-the-case-that-discrimination-is-bad-for-your-health

    Hersey, Tricia. "Rest is anything that connects your mind and body." *The Nap Ministry*. 21 Feb. 2021. https://thenapministry.wordpress.com/2022/02/21/rest-is-anything-that-connects-your-mind-and-body/

    Johnson, Traci. "Jenga for Life: What's at Play in Maternal Mortality." *2021 Maternal and Infant Health Convening*. The Uplift Connection, 28 Sept. 2021. Virtual Lecture. https://theupliftconnection.secure-platform.com/a/gallery/rounds/1/schedule/items/7

    Wamsley, Laurel. "Erica Garner, Who Became An Activist After Her Father's Death, Dies." *The Two Way*, NPR, 30 Dec. 2017. https://www.npr.org/sections/thetwo-way/2017/12/30/574514217/erica-garner-who-became-an-activist-after-her-fathers-death-dies

ACKNOWLEDGEMENTS

Huge shoutout to my family and friends for keeping me afloat throughout the years and filling my heart with joy. I would like to thank my dad for being my righthand man and supporting me through every up and down and in all my endeavors. To my Granny and Grandpa, thank you for being my biggest fans, I love you dearly. To Rita, Eric, Kayla, Will and Rheanna, thank you for loving me through every mood swing and breakdown. I love y'all more than you know. To my gang of cousins, all of my amazing Aunties and my Uncle Army, you are my heart. To Miss Lisa, thank you for the continuous love and support you gave to my mom and continue to give me.

To Fatima, Logan, Tabitha, Dianne, Shelby, and Avery thank you for being true friends throughout the craziness that was college. To Sarah, my friend and doula sister, thank you for the amazing illustrations and always being a listening ear. To Naomi, thank you for being my friend and handling my art with care. To Joy J. and Miss Jasmin, thank you both for being a constant uplifting presence in my life. To Joi M., I remember you asking me how I was doing and breaking down in tears during the summer of 2018. That day I shared my idea for *Wildflower* with you over pizza, and you bought me a purple journal and synthetic purple wildflower shortly after. Thank you for believing in me and my vision since high school. To Shante, for holding space for me to laugh and cry and reminisce about my mom with you as I navigated WashU. AOML to my ship, thank you for your continuous support and love. To Aunya, for helping me to be gracious with myself always. And to Jewel, for always being my personal cheerleader. Thank you.

Thank you to my WU-SLam family! Many of these poems were written either in Inklings or during P-Crew. Thank you to Sabrina and Victoria for reading my work and giving such thorough and thoughtful reviews. Also, thank you to my Poetry 1 class at WashU for workshopping "Tongues," and to my instructor Irina Televeva for giving feedback on several of these poems. Huge thank you to M.K. Stallings of UrbArts and Elizabeth Chambers for nurturing me as a young writer and giving me space to perform in high school. Big thanks to the team at Fifth Ribb Publishing and EyeSeeMe Bookstore for helping me through every step of this process and making my vision come to life.

ABOUT THE AUTHOR

IBURA AYELE is a creative, birth doula, and reproductive justice advocate based in St. Louis, Missouri who has been writing ever since she could pick up a pen and scribble. She wrote her first book, *The Little Book of Self-Control*, at age 11 as a self-help guide for kids who often found themselves in trouble with their parents. Through participating in slam poetry throughout high school and college she began to hone her craft and find her voice. Wildflower is Ibura's first collection of poems.

Learn more at www.Ibura-Ayele.com.

www.ingramcontent.com/pod-product-compliance
Lightning Source LLC
Chambersburg PA
CBHW041152110526
44590CB00027B/4212